MR. MEMORY

OTHER POEMS

BOOKS BY PHILLIS LEVIN

POETRY

Temples and Fields

The Afterimage

Mercury

May Day

Mr. Memory & Other Poems

AS EDITOR

The Penguin Book of the Sonnet:
500 Years of a Classic Tradition in English

MR. MEMORY

OTHER POEMS

Phillis Levin

PENGUIN POETS

PENGUIN BOOKS

An imprint of Penguin Random House LLC
375 Hudson Street
New York, New York 10014
penguin.com

LIBRARY OF CONGRESS CATALOGING-IN-PUBLICATION DATA
Names: Levin, Phillis, author.
Title: Mr. memory : & other poems / Phillis Levin.
Description: New York, New York : Penguin, [2016] | Series: Penguin Poets
Identifiers: LCCN 2015042145 | ISBN 9780143128113 (softcover)
Subjects: | BISAC: POETRY / American / General.
Classification: LCC PS3562.E88966 A6 2016 | DDC 811/.54—dc23

Printed in the United States of America
1   3   5   7   9   10   8   6   4   2

Set in Janson MT
Designed by Ginger Legato

FOR JACK

and to the memory of
Elfie Raymond and Helen Harshman Shanewise

CONTENTS

We live only for a flash. Until the lacquer dries.

—TOMAŽ ŠALAMUN

The curling movement consequent on a single touch continues to increase for a considerable time, then ceases; after a few hours the tendril uncurls itself, and is again ready to act.

—CHARLES DARWIN

MR. MEMORY

&

OTHER POEMS

FAME

I will disappear
Into the sea and not be
Heard from: by moonlight
Rise up galloping upon
A blue horse born in my blood.

LENTEN SONG

That the dead are real to us
Cannot be denied,
That the living are more real

When they are dead
Terrifies, that the dead can rise
As the living do is possible

Is possible to surmise,
But all the stars cannot come near
All we meet in an eye.

Flee from me, fear, as soot
Flies in a breeze, do not burn
Or settle in my sight,

I've tasted you long enough,
Let me savor
Something otherwise.

Who wakes beside me now
Suits my soul, so I turn to words
Only to say he changes

Into his robe, rustles a page,
He raises the lid of the piano
To release what's born in its cage.

If words come back
To say they compromise
Or swear again they have died,

There's no news in that, I reply,
But a music without notes
These notes comprise, still

As spring beneath us lies,
Already something otherwise.

ANNE FRANK'S HIGH HEELS

Miep managed to snap them up for 27.50 guilders.
Burgundy-colored suede and leather . . .

—ANNE FRANK, *THE DIARY OF A YOUNG GIRL*, AUGUST 10, 1943

When Miep took us home with her
She held us up in the air,

Eye-level with those eyes
You may know, eyes spelling

Sorrow-girl, wait-for-me,
Happiness-around-a-corner-

One-day, hurry-back, don't-tell.
Two new hands took us in,

Skin cradling skin.
How empty we had been,

Only a little bit worn—
Not a penny, not a pebble

Dwelling within.
We became an altar,

An offering red as wine,
A wishing well.

She was made to carry us
Near and far,

We were made to bear
The pressure of her feet

In darkness, in light,
Their sweetness, their heat.

We were getting used to her.
Miep calls us a handsome pair.

DEMITASSE

(circa 1887–   )

You evaded the firestorm, reaching the shore
Of the New World long before, so nothing
To speak of has shaken you more than the rage

In my father's voice or my brother's infant fist
Shattering a pane of the china closet, leaving you
Unharmed (the shards swept away, the glass

Replaced in a day). Through it all you never
Were lifted, never filled, until at the close
Of the century I asked for you. A door

Opened: you were offered without a pang,
Without a story. No shape have I beheld
As finely wrought—but are you the craft

Of a human hand or a portal to splendor?
Burnt umber glazes my espresso,
I'm adrift yet home, my lip touching

Yours touching gold; and when I'm done
I peer over the brim to find a faded
Corona within. Your fluted pedestal

Gives you balance, you contain an eternity
Of sighs: at the bottom, where you taper
And the dregs settle, thick enough to muffle

Any cry, a blossom abides in the center
(Even when you are empty something is there).
Sometimes I study the scallops of your body,

Slipping my fingers along your contours,
Curious about your lineage, wondering
Who else marveled at your lightness, your near-

Transparency, turning you over then to see
The mark of your maker—a blue lamb
Standing by a gilded rose, its feet resting

On a slender line, a single brushstroke saying,
This is the earth that will hold whatever
Dwells here, this the border dividing above

From below; and under this line, in a cursive
Deliberate and free, run the letters telling
Where you became what you are:

You were born in a lull called peace
In a kiln in Meissen, from a mound of clay
In the river's mossy marsh. You were reborn

In Dresden, adorned by a master-painter
Of flowers that bloom in fire. You arrived
In a steamer trunk in New York Harbor.

You need no saucer, have no mate.
I will look after you and pass you on,
Hoping you stay for the last drop of the last
Day, the future for which you were made.

BURGUNDY SCARF

Undertone of dying leaf, marvel
Of a scarf lost on a walk long ago,
Later returning. Hand that made it
Gone. Hand of the boy for whom
It was made, for whom it was meant,
Alive, keeping it alive, passing it on.
Smoky. Worn. Hand accepting it
Mine, touching fabric of division,
Undulant woof of meaning, question
That cannot be asked. Tell me, Father,
Do you remember her still, the girl
Before my mother, who made it for you,
Knitting it day by day until it was done?
Why did you give it to me, for now
It is lost again on another walk
Across another lawn. Did you need it
To be gone, did you suffer
For this giving, did you hold the words
In check, and is that mine, too,
To believe that there are words behind
No words, mine to find no words
Behind them? And if it was easy
To give away and meant so little,
And she means nothing to you
Anymore, why did your fingers tremble
When you placed the wine-red scarf

Around my neck? Why did it take
So long for me to wear it, what is gone
Now that it's gone for good?

TO AN ASH ON A CRACKLING LOG

Little bat, gray rose, you quicken now,
    a pulse abloom,

Curling in on yourself embryonically
    and in a breath

Spinning up the flue,
    a gust away from floating free

Into a cloud whose ions hold
    eons of lovers at play, gazing

Upon earth as if falling
    were a myth, as if they

Weren't a breath away
    from spinning, dear dervish, like you.

MR. MEMORY

Am I right, sir?

—HITCHCOCK'S *THE 39 STEPS*

He was raised in a decent home
Ignoring the whims of nature,
But nothing he did could ease
The loneliness of his father,

Neutral in dress and manner,
Preaching by the evening fire
In thrall to a set of decrees
No reasonable Lord would deliver.

At what age he started to show
A knack for total recall
Isn't recorded, though clearly
His skill disturbed his teachers

Until, on closer inspection,
They saw they had nothing to fear.
That was a heyday for memory,
When learning by rote was in fashion

And a beating brought forgotten
Passages to mind: every schoolboy
Knew the sting of the ruler,
How sons must carry the future

Out of a burning wreck.
The name of Napoleon's horse,
Who built St. Paul's, the distance
From Winnipeg to Montreal—

Information routine to peculiar
He could retain, connecting
Trains of syllables that flowed
And sputtered. The need to be

Correct, to be patted on the head
By a man in uniform or any figure
With a stiff upper lip, fueled
A desire that terrified even Freud,

Perfection repeating itself
In a mirror. But how innocent
Memory stays, how well to the end
He behaves: an unassuming man,

Whose little moustache conjures
Chaplin or Hitler, in a breath
Reciting to a T the formula
Stored inside him, unable to know

If he is aiding the forces for good
Or the forces of brute power,
Who pose the same question—
Though when the bullet cuts into

His answer, only the good hold him
As he collapses, taking another
Breath to finish his task, to ask
"Am I right, sir?"

THE STROLLER

Odessa Steps, Eisenstein's BATTLESHIP POTEMKIN

And aren't we all like this at times,
Bumping helplessly down the stairs

Into a street surging with fire,
The one whose eyes were upon us

Out of control of the handle
Attached to our carriage?

Why are we shocked when
The glasses drop and the face

Of horror crowds the screen?
The reel crackles, there is

No end in sight,
Nowhere to flee.

We have seen them before,
People who look surprised

To have lived so long: open
An album, pass a wooden door.

Late summer, the quiet creatures
Scurrying through grass

    Know it's time to start over,
    Theirs a genesis we cannot reenter.

TABULA RASA

To see not herself in the mirror but the mirror itself,
Startled by starlings, darlings of the eye, apples
At home in their lunar glow, piano scales
Welling below, with nobody near except

This child determined to gaze at a surface unyielding
Yet ever-fluctuating, giving in to every whim of light,
Giving in not at all to her wish, her will to be
Unseen. And why did she want this? Though I

Am she I cannot tell, can only say
Her desire was born starkly, bare-boned and mute,
Tiptoeing, flagrant—to face a giant nothingness
Full of family secrets, icy, molten,

Taciturn, unknown. Look at her trying to steal
A look without getting caught in the glass,
Betrayed again by a sliver of flesh, a quiver of
Self-sight. Here is the bed of the mother and father,

Island of sheets and pillows, Persian blue velvet,
Apricot silk, here the bureau of many drawers
(In one, under a packet of letters, Trojans
Asleep in their wrappers), a comb and a brush

Waiting to touch the prince and princess, perfumes
Growing old in their vials, baroque filigree stems . . .
To see not myself in the mirror but the mirror
Itself, a white wolf with its pink tongue panting.

DANDELION

Ferocious flower
Cast out

Dent de lion

Wily traveller
Rooted in ruthlessness

Dent de lion

Dreaded survivor
Poisoned hunted speared

Dent de lion

Exile returning to rule
Legions of grass

Dent de lion

On a spur of the moment
Dallying with the wind

Dent de lion

Settling in
To make a new broadcast

Dent de lion

Broaching the dream-gate
Tail swaying

Dent de lion

Jagged leaf
Bearing the bite of your name

Dent de lion

Your mane a nebula
Born from galaxies of gold

Dent de lion

A gray pincushion
Holding numberless stars

QUESTION FOR THE TREES

Why do you lead me
To words as you motion to
Cloudbanks of silence?

ROAD TRIP THROUGH THE ROCKIES
INTERRUPTED BY A DREAM

She is older than the rocks among which she sits . . .

—WALTER PATER

I

When the landscape tore away
I saw the likeness of Mona Lisa:

She was as large as a mountain,
Was a mountain,
The one watching over us
Everywhere, always.

She filled a billowing
Ragged banner, her face
Intact, entire—
Light seeping through
From another world churning behind.

In the valley below
Pooled a river of light,
Cooling shadows on which
Other shadows had floated all day.

For some reason I couldn't stop weeping.

From the highest peak she reigned
Over patches of sheep,
An orphan cloud, bundles of hay.

II

The professor stood up
Without fanfare or name,
And as he made his way through
Meadow-grass to a podium
Awaiting him

The landscape fell back
Into place, covering her face
Almost completely,
Like a shade drawn
Almost completely,
So that anyone could see
Something else was there,

As if the sky above
The river below
Were a scene on a linen screen

Hiding another sky,
Another range of mountains.

III

"This was Nonna's mother,"
He exclaimed, pointing to the mountain:
"Here her daughter's daughter played
Long ago, in the valley below,
In the ambit of her gaze."

So now we knew who she was.

Or did he say "no one's mother"?
No one in particular
Or no one's in particular,
So everyone's anywhere everywhere.

We weren't supposed to have seen the face
Behind the face of the mountain.

IV

Scent of nightfall.

A chaos of caws.

V

Those crows, Jack says,

The only reason they're up there
Is to have fun:

Why else would they jump
From the ledge
And tumble down,

Grabbing onto each other's feet,

Letting the updraft carry them back
Onto the highest peak?

VI

Ribbons of light
Spilling from a cliff:

Unmoving face,
Ever-moving strands
Vanishing after unveiling
Whatever we saw, whatever it was
We knew all along.

VII

"I'm a grandmother," she tells us.
We learn she is from Singapore
As she pours us a pot of tea.

Her father did something bad,
And that is why she ran away to Calgary.

VIII

A great one,
Smaller, grayer, bluer:
Not many features
Because far away,

Not really smaller,
Just far away.

As we drive closer they appear
Less beautiful, more real
—Steeper, sharper, bleaker,

Scarred by the work of the sun.

Pockets of snow in a vault
Of shale, a gushing ravine,
A flock of sheep, bales of hay.

IX

And up there was my professor,
My giant dear professor.
Then Katya was there, Saša too,

Strong women, not strong at all
In the way of my grandmother,
Who by some force or fear
Had been petrified: Lena,
A stone beyond reach,
Born a spark of the living fire.

X

Aren't we still like the crows?
We are very like them
In our playing—from afar
Belonging to the mountain,

A speck a brushstroke away
From the bluest shadow,
Whose beginning is nowhere

In sight, an emanation
Without apparent source
As a stream has a source
Though the eye discerns

No line to follow
And the place, if found,
Is found by climbing near

Against reason, against nature,
A journey whose labor
Isn't worth it, if worth
Is measured in what has weight.

Could the weight of the world
Reside in the light
On a jagged mountain?

XI

She up there, out there,
Nonna's mother
Or no one's,

The great grand parent
Arising once again
Before us,

A rock among rocks
Watching over us as we play,

The crows having a time of it,
Gathering along the ledge
Far above.

BAYOU HAIKU

Egret on a cloud
reflected in the water:
singular | plural

LYRE

Because it hangs from the center of the sky,
I play there sometimes, too, far away
From you, forgetting to return
Until my own fluttering breath unsettles me

More than the spaces pulsing between stars.
For years I rose in dreams beyond
Earth's atmosphere: each night,
As I left the mother ship to bob along

The surface of the moon, the cord
Snapped and I drifted away, pulled into
An orbit from which I couldn't break free.

My hands reach up to grab the yoke:
It stretches down, arms glittering,
A few crumbs of creation following.

BLESSING IN DISGUISE

The rain came down, the sun came up, then
Of all things what followed followed: a blessing
That was a blessing in disguise. Though things

Don't work out sometimes, don't work at all
At times, they have a way of adding themselves
To a sum we cannot count or account for.

That fedora, those two-tone shoes,
An ivory-handled umbrella in the vestibule,
Even the rooster weathervane pointing

As it will—they are made, some claim,
In vain. But they survive us, they remain.
A bird on Thanksgiving doesn't need much

Dressing, dons no disguise, granting us
An unmixed blessing it isn't a shame
To count on. A phone call stops the monster

Chasing the dreamer, and a smoking toaster
Defers an obit folded in the paper at the door.
The war (we've begun to ask which one)

Was less than a blessing by far,
Later a quandary pondered, later still
What it was from the start, a quarry of parts

A full account couldn't cover, food
For the vultures, who show no disgust for
The raw number of blessings mounting, a pure

Feast (purity can come to this) on a field
Where no one lies untouched by the blessing
Of night, falling as it does, no blade of grass

Unfed by a blessèd drop of blood. Morning
Rises, a curtain opens, we stand undone by all
We recognize. But who at any time can tell

What it was, and in whose eyes,
The blessing in disguise, dressed as it was.

X-RADIOGRAPH

Massacre of the Innocents

—PIETER BRUEGEL THE ELDER

A woman is bending over
Something in the snow: it appears
To be an array of ham and cheese.
What is it doing there? Is she lifting her arms
In dismay, or uttering a prayer of gratitude?
Will the bounty be taken away
By the soldiers closing in, or has abundance
Fallen unbidden
From a bitter winter sky?

According to the X-ray, the winter
Is just as bitter
But there is no ham, no cheese, though that
Is what the naked eye sees.
It isn't hunger, it's not a day of plunder,
Something else is bringing her to her knees.
If you look a little closer, the shadow
Of an infant shows through: you can find
Many such shadows in the scene.

A soldier is herding women to a doorway,
Armored knights on stallions
Stand guard. At another door is a soldier
Seizing a child who hasn't been painted over
(Changed into a bundle or a loaf of bread).
A dog is barking, birds have fled,
Icicles hang from the eaves,
By a frozen pond a riderless horse
Rubs its head on a tree.

Over another bundle (another infant
Shadow) another woman grieves.

For a couple imploring a soldier
To spare a pale winged creature almost
As big as the daughter, whose father
Is pointing to her, read: "Take the girl
Instead of our baby son" (concealed
Under a goose—or is it a swan?—
About to have its neck slashed open).
A soldier pissing against a wall
Disguises nothing at all.

Men bearing lances spear a rooster,
Stabbing until the last of the flock is dead.
Women faint at the sight of a dying boar
(A boy newly born not long before).
A woman cradles a pitcher: if the man
Hovering near her seems thirsty,
Do not fear: he will not spill any water,
The pitcher isn't a pitcher, the deed
He must do has been done.

The plunder has begun: it is bringing
Various people to their knees.
That is what a naked eye
Sees (a mother and child in flight
Were partially lost when another side
Of the panel was cut down).
As for the faded pair of socks
In the snow, they are
A faded pair of socks in the snow.

AS IT HAPPENS

As it happens, there was nothing left, so much to do, a plethora
Of urgencies, an unguent unglued

As it happens, everyone who wanted something had nothing to gain,
Nothing to lose, given the plenitude, given the remorse

As it happens, somersaults on the grass were not prohibited,
Not exhibited, but not for the reasons you'd suspect

As it happens, the classical stance broke down, the stoic wept,
Theaters opened in gutters, the rats came out to applause

As it happens, the spectacle stuck in our throats, the aftermath
Burst through the branches and flared, matchsticks sizzled with rain

Lucky are they who sing without knowing the words, *so la ti do,*
Whatever the blasphemy, whatever the praise

BOY WITH A BOOK BAG

Father, forgiue them, for they know not what they doe.

—LUKE 23:34

He arrived weeks after school had begun,
A boy with a book bag, his gestures
Sluggish and clumsy, the bag too big
For a child to carry—holding what
We didn't know. And though
By the following morning he was gone
For good, and no one except the teacher
Uttered a word about him thereafter,
Mrs. Matarazzo only saying
Victor had been "transferred,"
The day he was with us something
Entered the room that wouldn't leave.
The light began to change, as it did
Every fall, but something new
Among us remained.

This was the year the radio blared
A crime I thought I could have done.
I wondered if I had an alibi,
But could think of none since I
Could be everywhere at once, inhabit
Any mind, occupy any pair of shoes.
But there was someone I couldn't be:
Victor, sitting close to me.

I don't remember the face of the girl
Who took me aside one day and said
That I killed Jesus, relaying the news
Matter-of-factly, without prologue
Or proof, the verdict clear.
I wasn't sure what she meant
Exactly, but didn't I already believe
That I was capable of anything,
However terrible or grand,
Invisibility at my command?
If I could be accused of killing Christ
Couldn't I be the person the police
Were in hot pursuit of for robbing
A bank at gunpoint in Paterson?
You may ask how a six-year-old
Imagines such a thing, but why not:
What is holding up a bank
Next to murdering Jesus?

Whether he appeared
Before those suspicions or later,
Victor's brief life in our class
Unleashed so sudden a force
That the awkward bearing

Of his body, his ridiculously serious
Leather book bag, his bland expression
And the mottled pallor of his skin
Form a picture summoned
By the sound of his perfectly
Old-fashioned, inappropriate name.
But his parents may have christened him
Without knowing he would win
Little more than their love,
His intelligence so limited that a room
Of first graders learning to spell
Could tell right away he didn't belong.

Who did belong? I certainly stuck out,
A strange bird taller than all
The boys and all the girls, afraid to play
Because I didn't know that play
Was all in play. Ordinarily
I shared a desk with David Unger,
My true partner, the two of us
Pretending we were butchers
Trimming the fat off slabs of meat
We made of clay: dear David,
Who doodled in his copybook blissfully
What turned out to be equations

Of trigonometry, perplexing
Even the librarian with his questions.

On this day we were gathered round
A low Formica table, with Victor
Seated among us: the teacher
Led him over after pronouncing
His name. There must have been
A lull, a few minutes of quiet between
Handing in homework and beginning
Another lesson, when we were left
To ourselves. As if responding to a sign,
One child then another reached
Across to the place on the table
Where Victor's right hand
Was resting, and one by one,
With quick jabs, started pinching him.
He didn't cry out, they didn't stop.
Soon everyone had taken a turn
But me: then I too lifted my hand,
Reaching into the ring, but it
Wouldn't go further, it hovered
Above his, unable
To descend. A sensation arose,
Akin to the pressure created

When trying to bring together
Like magnetic poles.

                    Then it was over.
All at once Mrs. M. was there,
Standing above us, comprehending
What occurred. Pink blotches
And a trail of crescent moons from
The fingernails of children digging in
Covered the back of his hand.
I recall her silence (no reprimand).

They had watched and waited,
And he had watched and waited, too,
For a moment looking up at me
As if in my eyes he could read
What I would do. But I would be
The one who hesitated,
Mute as my useless hand in the air
Refusing to leave a mark on his skin,
Who would not partake of his flesh
Yet could not prevent the slaughter,
Who must atone for
Doing nothing to save him, saying
Nothing to save him, failing him,

Failing to join the others
In sin (they will be forgiven),
Condemned to an island
Of goodness, thereafter to see
The sad look of surprise in his
Uncurious eyes, his hand a lame
Bloated bird, their hands dipping in
For the kill, mine still among them.

Feared her, didn't we,
Didn't know why, pitied her, too,
Feared our pity, didn't know
Where it came from,

Where she came from,
Going daily down the block,
Pale skin, white shirt, dark hair,
Never stopping to look

Or say hello, passing door
After door—her pace odd
Only in its unwavering,
A gait steady, resolute, hers

Alone, her name unknown:
White shirt, dark hair, pale skin
Same time each morning,
Walking one sure line to

Who knows where.
Something about the thickness
Of her neck, how at the nape
Stray curls gathered,

Something in her gaze
Always looking forward, a bit
Downward, as if following
The angle of the earth:

Not a girl anymore,
Not a woman either, age
Indeterminate: black hair,
White skin, clean shirt,

Nothing to fear, same time
Each morning, unmistakable,
Plain as day, walking
One sure line, hers alone.

"ALIVE I WAS—I DIDN'T SPEAK A BIT"

Translated from the Anglo-Saxon
Riddle 39 (K-D 65)

Alive I was—I didn't speak a bit; even so, I die.
Once I was, I am again: everyone ravages me,
holds me tight and shears my head,
tears into my bare body, breaks my neck.
I wouldn't bite a man unless he bit me;
so many of them bite me.

HIS HANDS ON THE TABLE

His hands on the table before me. Large.
He who later was mine. Then not. Never mine,
Though I was his. Never his. Together in this
Because there were no words, only a bed

On which, a day on which, many days,
His or mine. Rain or shine. No walks, only
The room where it happens because it must,
Call it what you will, neither called it anything

At all, gave only everything to those hours
Until a word wanted to be said, and he heard
And fled. Returning after a pause to start again

As if there'd been no pause, knowing underneath
The word was near, wishing it could sleep
Between them as it lay awake between them.

ZENO BEGINS TO CONCLUDE

About certain things Zeno is certain:
it is not a good idea
to lie in a hammock made of nothing;

likewise,
no matter how one applies oneself
to any daily task,
it is hard to hang a clothesline between stars,

and this is true even more so in the morning,
when one wants to wake
to a clean sheet
but the only clean sheets are the clouds.

With this
one must
make do.

ZENO'S NURSE RECALLS HIS BIRTH

It took a long time   no time at all
There was a cry between patches of light
His mother rested laughing by
The starry sphere of his skull

Sliding into day he opened his eyes like any other
Speechless thing
Without hesitation he wiggled his toes
No evidence of anything set him apart

The swaddling cloth was especially fine
A swarm of questions formed in his father's mind
None of them found an answer
No one needed to find one that day

Pretty soon he was lost in a cavity of thought
Looking back it is easy to see it was in the dice
Pretty soon she carried all he ever was
Pretty soon he carried all he ever was

ZENO'S DREAM

deeper into zero Zeno
fell in a dream
until he woke praising everything

moving from one thing to another
by praising
one thing then another by moving

his body noticing his body
going forward
his hands his arms his legs

his hope rising
without weight or measure
a fleck of ash a flake of snow

iotas holding on
to naught

ZENO BREAKS HIS FAST

Water drop. Clink of a bottle. Crumb
From yesterday's guttering candle.
Hieroglyphs of grain in a cup,
Oblong bubble in the loaf

He tears apart. Sooner or later, it all
Adds up: profligate seeds studding
A split fig, infinitude in a jot of jam,
Pyramid in a crystal of salt.

He will put a few olives in a bowl,
Lift a lump of cheese from a barrel
Of brine, discover a spring

In the shadow of Aetna's crater
Muttering the riddle of one and many,
Substance unchanging, never at rest.

TENDRIL

Incandescent coil,
Light by which we read the light

Spiraling through you—

Nimble filament, by touch
Renewed, by touch commencing.

Muir Woods

LITHUANIA

in memory of Jean Blecker Levin

Not a trace, those days, not a sign
On a map of where you were from,
That farm greener than green

Rolling hills, hay high as a barn
Under skies without end, joy
Rolling, too, the way it used to.

Now that you're gone,
Lithuania reappears.

•

Not a map in the world
Will show where you are,
Now that you are long gone

Under the glowing ground,
Lending yourself to the grass,
Joined at last by Joe, who cried,

As they lowered you down,
"Jenny, my love, my life."

•

Wherever you are, being
Nowhere, show me a way
To be here, you who are gone

Into bottomless loam: ivy
Climbing the walls of waking,
The walls of sleep, show me

Two on a porch waiting
To see the flesh of their flesh.

BARCAROLLE

Belle nuit, ô nuit d'amour,
Souris à nos ivresses,
Nuit plus douce que le jour,
Ô belle nuit d'amour!

Over time it was forgotten, the box for ballet shoes, a carrying case with a separate compartment for one's tutu, for me and the other girls in my dance class an itchy orange skirt with orange and green polka dots on the bodice (to this day those colors together make me ill). After ballet lessons ceased, it stayed in my bedroom closet untouched. For how many years? Patent leather, black or red; cannot be sure. It's the sheen I recall, and the scent of plastic—wholesome, pleasing; and the thrill of running my fingers over the small appliquéd felt design on the cover. Something to carry with pride if you were proud. The narrow compartment for shoes, a chute to slip them into after the lesson was done, seemed like a secret door. The lessons, intended to cultivate grace, made me feel too tall and clumsy. But the case I loved.

Inside the main compartment was a mirror, and some-where behind that compartment was a music box no one could see. Undoing the snap, opening that flap, and folding the cover back meant looking into the mirror and starting the music. A tiny ballerina in a white tulle skirt, arms lifted up, toes en pointe, spun around, then stopped. She and the music resumed if the box was closed and opened. A mechanism completely hidden triggered the motion and the music. The melody was the Barcarolle from Offenbach's *Tales of Hoffmann*, a song I rec-ognized, notes my father played on the piano, sounding sorrowful and sure, staying with me whether or not the case was open. Not a song I heard in the house anymore; father stopped playing altogether one day, a minor altercation the cause, something involving the piano tuner.

The case remained in the closet, buried with other boxes, other things, the ballerina motionless, the music dormant. Lost for how many years? Until one night I was startled from sleep by the sound of a melody coming from somewhere inside my room, not from anywhere outside. It was the Barcarolle. I lay there in amazement, in terror, thinking a stranger had entered my room and was hiding behind the closet door. I could tell that the sound was coming from there. I sat up, frozen, considering what to do, knowing the only way to end my fear would be to open the door and say to whoever was there, "Kill me, kill me if you want to."

Those were the words I rehearsed before rising from bed. My parents were asleep, I did not want to awaken or frighten them. And what could my little brother do? I pulled open the closet door, I spoke that ridiculous line to a clutter of darkness. No one emerged, the music continued. I turned on a light. I hunted for the source of the sound, which stopped and started again. Then I saw what it was: the ballet case. Somehow, among piles of books and clothing and shoes about to be moved when we moved to another house, everything had slowly shifted, the dance case, too, and in this shifting the case had opened slightly and music asleep for years began to play, the mechanism working, though faltering, repeating the song rather than letting it end. I closed the case. I closed the closet door. I went back to bed.

I married a man who plays the Barcarolle. Hearing that music long ago, I never thought it needed words; words get in the way. Now that I know them the night is sweet, though not much sweeter than day.

The only icon I've ever prayed to
Is you, a dapper man I never knew:
Because you died, your daughter
Longed for you so completely
There wasn't room for anything

To bloom. No place for my father,
Handsome man, good provider,
Overshadowed by your shadow
And a sullen shade, the woman
You wed, who carried a key

To lock every door. Come back,
Come back to us, please, I'd implore,
So everything can be all right again:
They will marry and live on their own
With no one watching them, and I

And then my brother will be born.
Your portrait sits on the drum table
Still, the frame cold to the touch,
Your eyes a pale tinge of the Baltic Sea,
Your mouth an unreadable line

Keeping a silence unlike my father's,
Which breaks from time to time
When he sings from out of the blue
Do not forsake me, oh my darlin'
Rejoicing in a sorrow unbound.

GULF

Imagine a dot
On the horizon: that is
Him, your beloved.

•

Imagine a dot
On the horizon: that is
Not your beloved.

•

A dot flickers on
The horizon: pilot light
For the beloved.

•

A dot with a name
Hovers on the horizon:
Here, gone, there, gone, here.

•

Imagine a dot
On the horizon: here then
Gone then him then her.

CLOUD FISHING

To fish from a cloud in the sky
You must find a comfortable spot,
Spend a day looking down
Patiently, clear-sighted.

Peer at your ceiling:
Where a light dangles, hook & line
Could be slipping through.

Under the hull of a boat
A fish will see things this way,

Looking up while swimming by—

A wavering pole's refraction
Catching its eye.

What will you catch?
With what sort of bait?
Take care or you'll catch yourself,

A fish might say,
As inescapable skeins of shadow
Scatter a net
Over the face of the deep.

SUMMER STUDY

I'd been loafing about in the loam,
Reading the cryptogams, that sexless
Tome of lichen, fern, and moss,
After lifting the veil sepulchring

A lone pinecone in the dew-studded,
Rainbow-freckled grass the morning
I left home for a walk somewhere
To find what I wasn't looking for.

There it was: a vine scaling a stone
Façade, firewood in the portico,
The invitation of an open door.

In the weave of a rug creatures
At play rested, with time at bay.
Enter, the eyes of a lion said.

DEAR MISS BISHOP,

Considering your words I must say I disagree
Wholeheartedly. Losing is impossible
To master, though it isn't hard to master

A certain tone, perfecting an art that *sounds*
Like it's making sense. It isn't. It's been
A year: as I look outside at bare branches

Stirred by a bird's random landing,
It only seems she is near—her voice
Clear, though I will not see her

Again (in a hollow trunk I found
Instead of emptiness a bluebell
Blue as her eye). Wherever she lived,

An ample forest flourished, a play
Of thought so thorough and free
Light on a leaf rekindles her laughter.

How natural it is to die, she taught me,
A motion of her hand showing the way
She comforted her old retriever,

Stroking Ginger's coat until her final
Breath. Broken and unbroken spines
Hold what I've read and mean to read,

But going back to something she said
Leads to a blind passage. Yet I rise
From my chair and move across a room

To call her still (I am about to lift
The receiver), knowing she'd rather talk
Face to face and will not want to stay

On the telephone. So with all due respect
I write today as one who, carrying wine
Or flowers or just herself, arrived

At Elfie's door—to be led to the lantern-
Glow of her table, a world unwritten
Beginning (*thou art*) to be spoken,
A listening always hungry for more.

for Elfie Raymond (1931–2012)

BATS IN THEIR PAVILION

World of Darkness, The Bronx Zoo

Upside down on a bare branch

They slept, some alone, some in pairs,
Notes composing a silent score.

So little going on besides our breath,

But something about them
Kept us there, leaning into each other,

Courting still. We had entered

The World of Darkness,
Seeking shelter from the midday sun,

When they appeared: at the end

Of a cool corridor, a tableau
Suspended in the glass separating

Our bodies from theirs.

How big some of them were—
A wing began to stir (why were four

Grasping feet peeking out

From a single creature?), opening
Enough for us to see

Another bat inside, hidden

Till then, asleep upside down
In the other. Another (and another)

Cape unfurled, showing each one

To be two:
One all along enfolded by the other,

Huddling to make their own weather.

MEMOIR

Within you will find many holes,
A passage that couldn't bear
To be read, couldn't bear to be
Missing, places torn, blotted out,
Undone by necessity.

Instead of a *this* only *that*, a naught
Over time increasing, a maturity, a
Burning away, a clearing, so to speak.
Fill it in as you will, it becomes a blind
Imagining, less than a world

Whose spiraling grasses and stars
Kept a secret alive, within reach
Of all who are kin,
Who increase, over time, this privacy,
Holding a candle to it as it multiplies.

On a day without day
This planet again will be stone,
A cavern without water or flesh, a skull
Devoid of countenance, anonymous,
Ready to express anything, including

Emptiness, the memento of a god
Whose eye sockets, once,
Were tunnels of love where someone
Such as yourself dwelled long ago—
I'm passing through one slowly

As possible now, there's so much to see
I do not want to reach the other side
(You know what I mean
If you followed me here somehow
With your hands, your eyes).

SCHIELE'S CHAIR

Flesh of the spirit,
The only one home finding
The only one home.

FROM A ROOFTOP

in memoriam: Tomaž Šalamun

From one little roof to another we leap,
The light is dark in between,
A darkness so bright
We should cover our eyes,
Leap without looking

Across or down, where you are
No more, only here and there
Under the crown
Always touching your name,
Gable in which a whisper lives on.

O Tomaž, is that a dove landing?
Or an arrowhead aimed at the zed,
Whose motor keeps purring?

Meadows and seas seek you out,
The grass cannot rest, the waves
Crave the shore, the crest of the tide
Cannot hide the trough
That you left by going too soon.

Wind whistles through the shutters:
Something is comforting someone,
Someone is saying, *Hush,*
There is no need to speak,
The end an illusion beginning to sing.

A roe in the forest shivers in sleep.
A solemn hunter raises his bow,
Sending an arrow to shoot a flake of snow.

Awake in wonder, dear friend,
In wonder we weep,
From the rooftops we call you,
One little roof to another
We leap—from ž to Š—

Crossing the narrow chasm
Between, space enough
For the seed of a linden
Or a bud of cyclamen
Uncurling like Metka's laughter.

Under the roof of the rain is your name,
Under the roof of your name you remain,
At the end of the very end two doves landing.

ANOTHER ROOM

There is another room
You could spend time in.
What a shame not to enter
More often: walls a color

Hard to imagine, windows
Overlooking a shy garden.
From there it is easy to see
A neighbor pinning laundry,

Composing a line of forlorn
Collars and sleeves
Punctuated by buttons
Catching the afternoon sun,

Whose face was a stranger
Until their mother-of-pearl
Was torn from a bed in a reef.
Whenever a chance to return

Returns, you wonder why
You didn't sit in that sofa,
Alone or near someone
In a chair, watching

A robin abandon
The swaying branches,
Listening to rain on the roof,
Undersong of comfort,

Undersong of grief.
A lifetime could be wasted
Dreaming there, a lifetime
Wasted not dreaming there.

The letters that must be taken away
To find the word nestled inside

Or not yet born. Removing those letters,
Deciding how many, which ones,

Is a science that resembles forgetting,
Dismemberment in the service of song.

Finally a new word rises from its shell,
And if it cannot rise it calls out, saying

It's time to be said, I've been here
All along, but you were reading with-

Out speaking, seeking without seeing
A syllable alone is a seed of light.

NOTES

The first epigraph is from "Lacquer" (translated by Tomaž Šalamun and Christopher Merrill) in Šalamun's collection *The Four Questions of Melancholy: New and Selected Poems* (White Pine Press, 1996). The second epigraph is from Charles Darwin's *On the Movements and Habits of Climbing Plants*, published in 1865 in the *Journal of the Linnean Society of London (Botany)*.

"ANNE FRANK'S HIGH HEELS"

Miep Gies (1909–2010), born Hermine Santruschitz in Austria, was a Dutch citizen who began working for Otto Frank in 1933, the same year the Frank family moved to Amsterdam. She befriended the family and helped hide them from the Nazis. After they were arrested, Miep retrieved Anne's diary and kept it safe; she gave it to Otto Frank in 1945, when he returned from Auschwitz and informed her of Anne's death. The poem's epigraph is from *The Diary of a Young Girl: The Definitive Edition*, edited by Otto H. Frank and Mirjam Pressler, translated by Susan Massotty (Random House, 1997).

"DEMITASSE"

In 1887 the Dresden porcelain painter Ambrosius Lamm founded the workshop where the cup evoked here was decorated; blanks were made in Meissen. Lamm's initial mark, a blue lamb above the word *Dresden* spelled out in script, was used between 1887 and 1890. His studio became one of the leading workshops in Europe for decorative wares; it was severely damaged in the October 1944 Allied bombing raid, finally closing in 1949.

"MR. MEMORY"

Questions posed to Mr. Memory are drawn from Alfred Hitchcock's 1935 film *The 39 Steps* and from the script by Patrick Barlow for a stage version that premiered in 2005. Hitchcock based his film on John Buchan's novel *The Thirty-Nine Steps* (1915), but radically altered the narrative by introducing Mr. Memory into the plot. Mr. Memory's character was modeled on William James Maurice Bottle (1875–1956), known as "Datas, the Memory Man," who performed in London theaters and music halls when Hitchcock was young.

"DANDELION"

The name of the plant, deriving from *dent de lion* (Middle French), "tooth of a lion," refers to the shape of its leaves.

"X-RADIOGRAPH"

When Pieter Bruegel the Elder painted *The Massacre of the Innocents* (circa 1565–67), he gave the story in St. Matthew's Gospel a contemporary context. X-radiography reveals that the scene originally depicted Spanish troops and their German mercenaries killing the children of a Flemish village; by 1621 the canvas had been altered to suggest an act of plunder, with animals and household objects concealing the infants underneath. The painting's first known owner, Rudolf II Habsburg, King of Hungary and Bohemia, and Holy Roman Emperor, was probably responsible for having the painting altered. The painting was acquired by Charles II in 1662 and is in the Royal Collection, the King's Dressing Room, Windsor Castle.

"BARCAROLLE"

The lines comprising the epigraph are from the barcarolle song in Jules Barbier's libretto for *Les Contes d'Hoffmann* by Jacques Offenbach.

"DEAR MISS BISHOP,"

This epistle to Elizabeth Bishop alludes to the opening lines in her poem "One Art."

"BATS IN THEIR PAVILION"

World of Darkness was a pavilion of nocturnal creatures at the Bronx Zoo, a permanent exhibition that opened in 1969 and closed in 2009 for fiscal reasons. Animals housed in that space were transferred to various other zoos in the United States.

"FROM A ROOFTOP"

The Slovenian word for the caron (or haček), the diacritical mark that looks like an inverted circumflex, is *strešica*, meaning "little roof."

ACKNOWLEDGMENTS

The author wishes to thank the editors of the following journals and anthologies in which these poems, sometimes in slightly different form, first appeared:

AGNI: "Blessing in Disguise," "To an Ash on a Crack-
ling Log"

Alhambra Poetry Calendar 2016: "Fame"

Barrow Street: "Bayou Haiku," "Schiele's Chair," "Zeno
Begins to Conclude," "Zeno's Dream," "Zeno's
Nurse Recalls His Birth"

Kenyon Review: "Burgundy Scarf"

Miramar: "Dear Miss Bishop,"

The New Criterion: "Zeno Breaks His Fast"

The Ocean State Review: "Mr. Memory," "Question for
the Trees," "To a Gentleman in Monochrome"

The Paris-American: "Bats in Their Pavilion"

The Paris Review: "Another Room," "Dandelion," "Gulf"

Plume: "As It Happens," "Lyre," "On Either Side of the
Word Lie"

Poetry: "Anne Frank's High Heels," "Cloud Fishing,"
"Lenten Song"

Poetry London: "From a Rooftop," "Summer Study,"
"Tabula Rasa"

Poetry Northeast: "His Hands on the Table"

The Poetry Review: "Boy with a Book Bag"

Southwest Review: "Barcarolle"

TAB: The Journal of Poetry & Poetics: "Slow"

Tikkun: "Demitasse"

Transom: "Memoir" (under the title "Journal")

The Yale Review: "Road Trip Through the Rockies
Interrupted by a Dream"

"Alive I Was—I Didn't Speak a Bit" appears in *The Word Exchange: Anglo-Saxon Poems in Translation*, edited by Greg Delanty and Michael Matto (W. W. Norton, 2012).

"Burgundy Scarf" and "Zeno Breaks His Fast" were featured on *Poetry Daily* as poems of the day.

"Lenten Song" is reprinted in *The Poet's Quest for God: 21st Century Poems of Faith, Doubt, and Wonder*, edited by Oliver Brennan, Todd Swift, Dominic Bury, and Cate Myddleton-Evans (Eyewear Publishing, 2016); "Lenten Song" also appeared in the "Poetry Pairings" feature of the *New York Times* Learning Network.

"Lithuania" was published in the Poem-A-Day program, an online feature sponsored by the Academy of American Poets.

"The Stroller" appears in *The Plume Anthology of Poetry 3*, edited by Daniel Lawless (MadHat Press, 2015).

Immense gratitude as ever to Molly Peacock and to Christopher Ricks, Jack Shanewise, Elizabeth Spires, and Rosanna Warren for their encouragement and criticism. I wish to thank Hofstra University for granting a special leave crucial to the completion of this collection and The Brewster Inn for its hospitality during the time some of these poems were written. Special thanks to Paul Slovak for his unerring advice and support.

Phillis Levin is the author of four other poetry collections, *Temples and Fields* (1988), *The Afterimage* (1995), *Mercury* (2001), and *May Day* (2008). She is also the editor of *The Penguin Book of the Sonnet* (2001). Her honors include the Poetry Society of America's Norma Farber First Book Award, a Fulbright Scholar Award to Slovenia, the Amy Lowell Poetry Travelling Scholarship, a Bogliasco Fellowship, and grants from the Ingram Merrill Foundation, the Guggenheim Foundation, and the National Endowment for the Arts. Widely anthologized, her work has appeared in *The New Yorker, The Atlantic, Grand Street, Poetry, The Paris Review, Kenyon Review, Southwest Review, The Yale Review, PN Review, New Republic, AGNI, Poetry Review, Poetry London*, and *The Best American Poetry*. Born in Paterson, New Jersey, Levin holds degrees from Sarah Lawrence College and The Johns Hopkins University. She has taught at the University of Maryland at College Park, the Unterberg Poetry Center, and New York University, and currently is a professor of English and poet-in-residence at Hofstra University. She lives with her husband, Jack Shanewise, in New York.

PENGUIN POETS

JOHN ASHBERY
Selected Poems
Self-Portrait in a
Convex Mirror

PAUL BEATTY
Joker, Joker, Deuce

TED BERRIGAN
The Sonnets

LAUREN BERRY
The Lifting Dress

PHILIP BOOTH
Lifelines: Selected Poems
1950–1999

JULIANNE BUCHSBAUM
The Apothecary's Heir

JIM CARROLL
Fear of Dreaming:
The Selected Poems
Living at the Movies
Void of Course

ALISON DEMING
Genius Loci
Rope

CARL DENNIS
Another Reason
Callings
New and Selected Poems
1974–2004
Practical Gods
Ranking the Wishes
Unknown Friends

DIANE DI PRIMA
Loba

STUART DISCHELL
Dig Safe

STEPHEN DOBYNS
Velocities: New and Selected
Poems, 1966–1992

EDWARD DORN
Way More West

ROGER FANNING
The Middle Ages

ADAM FOULDS
The Broken Word

CARRIE FOUNTAIN
Burn Lake
Instant Winner

AMY GERSTLER
Crown of Weeds
Dearest Creature
Ghost Girl
Medicine
Nerve Storm
Scattered at Sea

EUGENE GLORIA
Drivers at the Short-Time
Motel
Hoodlum Birds
My Favorite Warlord

DEBORA GREGER
By Herself
Desert Fathers, Uranium
Daughters
God
Men, Women, and Ghosts
Western Art

TERRANCE HAYES
Hip Logic
How to Be Drawn
Lighthead
Wind in a Box

NATHAN HOKS
The Narrow Circle

ROBERT HUNTER
Sentinel and Other Poems

MARY KARR
Viper Rum

JACK KEROUAC
Book of Blues
Book of Haikus
Book of Sketches

JOANNA KLINK
Circadian
Excerpts from a Secret Prophecy
Raptus

JOANNE KYGER
As Ever: Selected Poems

ANN LAUTERBACH
Hum
If in Time: Selected Poems,
1975–2000
On a Stair
Or to Begin Again
Under the Sign

PHILLIS LEVIN
May Day
Mercury
Mr. Memory & Other Poems

PATRICIA LOCKWOOD
Motherland Fatherland
Homelandsexuals

WILLIAM LOGAN
Macbeth in Venice
Madame X
Strange Flesh
The Whispering Gallery

ADRIAN MATEJKA
The Big Smoke
Mixology

MICHAEL MCCLURE
Huge Dreams: San Francisco
and Beat Poems

ROSE MCLARNEY
Its Day Being Gone

DAVID MELTZER
David's Copy: The Selected
Poems of David Meltzer

ROBERT MORGAN
Dark Energy
Terroir

CAROL MUSKE-DUKES
An Octave above Thunder
Red Trousseau
Twin Cities

ALICE NOTLEY
Culture of One
The Descent of Alette
Disobedience
In the Pines
Mysteries of Small Houses

WILLIE PERDOMO
The Essential Hits of Shorty
Bon Bon

LIA PURPURA
It Shouldn't Have Been Beautiful

LAWRENCE RAAB
The History of Forgetting
Visible Signs: New and Selected
Poems

BARBARA RAS
The Last Skin
One Hidden Stuff

MICHAEL ROBBINS
Alien vs. Predator
The Second Sex

PATTIANN ROGERS
Generations
Holy Heathen Rhapsody
Wayfare

ROBYN SCHIFF
A Woman of Property

WILLIAM STOBB
Absentia
Nervous Systems

TRYFON TOLIDES
An Almost Pure Empty Walking

SARAH VAP
Viability

ANNE WALDMAN
Gossamurmur
Kill or Cure
Manatee/Humanity
Structure of the World
Compared to a Bubble

JAMES WELCH
Riding the Earthboy 40

PHILIP WHALEN
Overtime: Selected Poems

ROBERT WRIGLEY
Anatomy of Melancholy and
Other Poems
Beautiful Country
Earthly Meditations: New and
Selected Poems
Lives of the Animals
Reign of Snakes

MARK YAKICH
The Importance of Peeling
Potatoes in Ukraine
Unrelated Individuals Forming
a Group Waiting to Cross